(Better) With Salt & Pepper

Nidhi Patel

BookLeaf
Publishing

(Better) With Salt & Pepper © 2022 Nidhi Patel

All rights reserved.

No part of this publication may be reproduced, stored in a retrieval system, or transmitted, in any form or by any means, electronic, mechanical, photocopying, recording or otherwise, without the prior written permission of the presenters.

Nidhi Patel asserts the moral right to be identified as author of this work.

Presentation by *BookLeaf Publishing*

Web: www.bookleafpub.com

E-mail: info@bookleafpub.com

ISBN: 978-93-95890-18-2

First edition 2022

To my friends, for always being my most honourable critics.

ACKNOWLEDGEMENT

I shall acknowledge the vast amount of time invested by my best friend, Mahi Patel. For always being there to provide me with honest feedback. Then helping me come up with better ideas to write about; I couldn't have gotten to this day without you. Without you tolerating me every time I bugged you to review my work.

The Envious Bird

It's that time of the year again.
Spring is almost over summer is just around the
corner.
All over the land is filled with greenery.
Every flower is blooming every tree is coming
alive.
The view is breathtaking from my cage of silver.
Although, I do despise it very much.
I wish for something much more glamorous.
Often I've wished for a cage of gold.
One that glistens when the sun shines on it.
Often I've wished for my cage to change, as do
the seasons.
I want to be the envy of the land, one like no
other.
I await my golden cage.
Many days have passed.
Nature's miracle has gifted me a golden cage;
One just like I hoped for.
It is finally spring, once again.
A million birds flutter across the horizon line.
Each one spread out in a different direction, like
fireworks on display.
Something tugged at my heart;
And suddenly, I started hating my cage of gold.

I wanted to fly, fly higher than the sky.
I want to fly in and out of the horizon.
I want to break free from this cage.
I want to be free like the others.
Somewhere out in the distance, a big blast sounds.
The horizon is mostly clear except for a few birds here and there.
One by one, the birds plummet toward the ground faster than the speed of light.
And I knew the sound was of birds being shot.
Relief washes over me with the realization I was much safer in this golden cage of mine than anywhere else.
I cherish this gift of safety.
I think of how lucky I am to have it.
I think about how lucky I am to have a home, all to myself.
And I realize silver or gold.
In the end, they both protect me the same.
I knew there was no other luxury than the gift of safety.

The End

I walked through a path of thorns,
To get to the beds of flowers.
Only to find the petals wilted with decay;
And I knew, in that instance, that this was it.
This was the end of the story we began so long
ago;
And yet it will remain unfinished even though
we have reached the end.

Matters Of The Heart

It's not that I have forgotten.
I still think of you each time.
But the distance is so much between us.
I fear that doing so might be a crime.

I wish we could talk about things like we did
before.
But every single time, I stop before I send that
text.
Not a day goes by when I am not reminded of
the days that have passed.
The thought of what we have become is still
something that leaves me perplexed.

Every day is a ray of new hope, and each night
brings the same disappointment.
It surprises me to think how we could let
something so precious slip away.
If I had just one wish, I would ask for you.
I would make a promise, even if it's hard to
keep, to never let our ties fray.

Nature's Whisper

Often when they walk down paths of flowers
and fruits;
They heard little critters talking to trees and their
roots.
They will say they love you more than the birds
and bees that sit on your flower,
They don't tell you it will never be more than
themselves only; until you're needed, and
they're always in power.

The message carried down the streams to the
rivers, lakes, and oceans.
When the ocean heard the news, it roared in
angry motions.
When the hikers passed by, they stopped for a
moment, missing the ocean when it was full of
salty water.
Now all they got are a bunch of salty tears; and a
welcoming wave turned tauter.

The ocean and the sky were best friends.
It was so where the ocean died, was where the
sky transcends.
The sky was moody, changing colours as the
days, go by.

The stars envied its beauty as they let out a
jealous sigh.

They burned in a fury, destroying everything in
the way.
Little did they know there would be a hefty price
to pay.
When galaxies far away began to cry in pain.
They realized their victory was nothing but a
disgraceful stain.

Good Bye

I'm finally understanding; what the meaning of
goodbye is.
From what I'm gathering, it seems,
It's that love you thought was going to last
forever.
The one that you expect will always be true.
It will make you feel safe and secure.
Strong enough to dream;
But vulnerable enough to make up scenarios that
are never going to happen.
Vulnerable enough; to bring every dream
crashing to the floor in the blink of an eye.
The problem is not that we dream too much.
The problem is we dream too much but of the
wrong person.
You will wait forever and for as long as it may
take expecting things to change.
You will move from place to place, leaving
pieces of you everywhere you go.
All for that one's happiness;
Because you made them your priority.
They taught you that you stand below them.
So when it is time for you to live your dreams,
You couldn't remember what loving yourself
was like;

You couldn't remember when someone tells you;
that you stand before anyone.
That your happiness, comes over everything in
the world.
You don't understand these things.
And when you go home,
You will be sobbing into your pillow.
You will be wondering where you went wrong.
Covering your face with makeup the very next
morning, trying to hide the darkness under your
eyes;
Since you are pretty old now;
And this isn't your first heartbreak.
You will go about your life pretending nothing
ever went wrong while you slowly die inside.
When you smile in the mirror while wearing
your favourite lipstick, you suddenly feel like it
disgraces your face.
You will slit your wrists.
Let the blood pour down the tub inside the
locked bathroom.
As you close your eyes for the last time, the only
thought that will come to your mind;
To hope you find someone who loves you
enough to make you never want to leave.
But if you do, know that I will always be here
watching over you, looking out for you.

They Won't Tell You

I hope someone tells you this one day.
You think people don't notice you, putting up
barriers, fading in and out of the dark.
Believing your own lies, you are no master of
disguise.
For every place I go, I do find your mark.
The day I found you, you stood smiling in the
spotlight.
I knew how scared you were, and your fear was
inevitable when I tried to come close.
But the way you looked at me, I knew.
I had to get you out of that pose.
Of course, I warned you.
The more you pull away, the closer I will come,
I tell you;
Give me your hand;
I will never let you go.
Let me help you find reasons to smile, even just
a few.
If I was the crackling thunder; up above, you
were the calm ocean floor down below.
Without you, I was nothing; together, we were
everything.
Your one tear and every silence break my world
apart.

But when you smile, every star in my sky is
shining.
Of course, I would never tell you these things;
But if I ever did, I'd say.
My every wish to god asks for your safety;
To ask for the healing of your scars.
For you, I'd walk on fire.
For you, I'd go to war.
I will never stop trying until I break those bars.

Somewhere Far Away

Before you know it,
Your running;
To a faraway town.
Somewhere where you are unseen;
Hidden from the crowd.
A place too strange to call home;
And you know there is no turning back;
When you first arrive, you think it will be a new
start.
A brand new life;
In a brand new city.
You will be happy that you are finally alone.
Telling yourself; you are brave;
That no one can hurt you now.
No one can catch you.
But then, before you know it,
It will be four in the morning, and you will
struggle to fall asleep.
You will look toward your bottle of sleeping
pills on your night table,
It is no use; the bottle is now empty.
The last three pills that were there before,
Have already washed down your throat about an
hour ago;
And while you lay there thinking- silently.

Replaying; all the stories in your head.
Stories you tried to run away from;
When the air catches; in your lungs
The way it does when you run a marathon.
The sounds of your heart are louder than you can
bear to hear, to the point where you think you're
going deaf.
You feel like you've been running for too long;
And now it's about time to stop running, for
good.
Standing with your head held high, brave as you
always were and will be forever.

Behind Closed Eyes

Behind the doors of closed eyes,
I see fireworks exploding in the air.
A fire by the seashore;
Burning without care.

Some days I find myself in a jungle.
Swinging from vine to vine.
The next moment I am home,
Connecting stars line by line.

I run through rose fields.
The aroma chasing after me.
Flying in the sky with the birds;
Feeling free as could be.

Faces

In a crowd of people, we have never seen.
We look for places we might consider foreseen.

People walk by trying to hide who they are.
Oblivious to the fact that reality is too far.

With every step, we look for a new mystery.
We end up finding the same old history.

Yet we continue moving past the hues.
Carrying ignorance; and forgetting that we all
wear the same shoes.

Free

We took so much for granted; I hope you see.
It roars louder every day, calling out to me yet; I
have not looked at the sea.
The once blue waters are now a murky brown,
the colour of your stone eyes.
The colour of the water does not shock me once
time flies.
The book of my life is still open to the page
where you left it unfinished.
My lamp glows with a light still to this day,
waiting for you, undiminished.
Like a deep and dark stain of ink within the
pages.
The birds have flown from within their cages.
The sun is about to set.
I guess I have lost this bet.
I run across the sand following behind as the
sound of your laughter calls out to me.
Only to realize I have already set you free.

Deadly Rose

The rose is a gun,
Pointed straight at my heart.
A bullet that never fails to hit the target,
At any distance, near or apart.

A sweet pain spreads throughout me as,
The thorns slowly prick away at my heart.
The wall of ice that stood once unwavering lies
shattered on the ground.
It is truly a miracle and instantly a work of art.

The intruder has invaded the carefully guarded
kingdom,
I see myself giving in to the chaos as each guard
is taken down.
It is too late to win the battle now,
I, the queen, am captive within the captivator's
eyes, and now I shall surrender my crown.

Her Story

She wasn't lazy.
She was tired.
Of standing on a battlefield;
That she didn't want to be on.
She just wanted to go home.
To sleep in her big comfy bed that kills all her
nightmares.

Sounds Of Joy

I'm breathing.
I'm screaming.
I'm spreading colours everywhere.
I'm celebrating.

Escaper

If I had told you I had wings, you'd think I was
lying.
Maybe crazy even.
It's how I escape.
To faraway lands on blue-looking days;
Until I'm whole again.

Where They Were Sad

When I last saw you, you were like the flowers I
have always loved.
You were like the rosy pink petals that I liked to
tuck behind my ear when I wore that blue dress
of mine that you always loved.
Now you're like the wilted petals begging for
water.
Now you're like prickly thorns that make me
bleed.
Yet, I keep trying to reach you; but you're just
not the same.

Innocence

21

This heart loves things too easily;
It goes after things it was never destined for.
Flying over galaxies and walking paths made of
burning coal.
Pricking edges over broken tea cups.
In search of the end of the rainbow;
To be stranded and alone on deserted paths.

Snow

I used to be the rain on cool summer nights;
Pattering on windows and running down roofs.
I used to make the flowers giggle with my touch.
Now I am snow on cold winter mornings;
An icicle, sharper than a dagger.
I am the deadly touch of frostbite.

Infinity

I wish I had spent time with you when I had the
chance.
We could have dreamed of going to Italy
together or to France.

Maybe walk through flower fields or over snowy
hills.
Only I know how much this distance kills.

In this world, we might not have been meant to
be.
Yet in a parallel universe, there is no you or I but
only we.

The First Meeting

A whirlwind of emotions,
A heart full of hope.
A mind full of chaos,
A Feeling of restlessness.
And when the two souls come together,
They burst into fireworks in the sky.

Missing Part

You're a part of me I never want to let go.
You're a part of me I never want to change.
The shore on the beach, I keep coming back to
no matter how far I go.
Separated from each other, yet unseparated.
I'll hold on to you as the sun holds on to the sky;
And I will always hope you stay holding my
hand.
Closer to your heart.
For as long as we live;
Stop me when I refuse to stay.
Look into my eyes, and I'll look into yours,
tears streaming down our faces;
And tell me that we can fight the world.
Together like one soul, one heart, one life.

You Play Bad Games

Ever since you left, nothing has been the same.
I don't know what this glory is or this fame.
It seems that for you, it was all just a game.
Darling, the move you have just made is nothing
but lame.

www.ingramcontent.com/pod-product-compliance
Lightning Source LLC
LaVergne TN
LVHW021338200726

843509LV00014B/2561